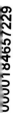

CEREAL
CITY GUIDE
COPENHAGEN

ABRAMS IMAGE,
NEW YORK

A City Guide by C E R E A L

Rosa Park, Editor in Chief
Rich Stapleton, Creative Director
Ruth Ainsworth, Sub Editor
Ollie Horne, Assistant Editor
Charlie Cook, Editorial Intern
Lily Dalzell & Molly Cropper,
Producers

Book design by
Studio Faculty

Photography by
Ash James, Chris Tonnesen,
Martin Kaufmann, Rich Stapleton,
Toby Mitchell

Illustrations by
Jessica Ng

Words by
Lucy Brook, Nana Hagel,
Nikolaj Hansson, Ollie Horne,
Aslan, Ruth Ainsworth

Editor: Laura Dozier
Managing Editor: Glenn Ramirez
Design Manager: Danny Maloney
Production Manager: Katie Gaffney

Library of Congress Control Number:
2020931086

ISBN: 978-1-4197-4714-4
eISBN: 978-1-68335-997-5

Printed and bound in China
10 9 8 7 6 5 4 3 2 1

Abrams books are available at special discounts when purchased in quantity for premiums and promotions as well as fundraising or educational use. Special editions can also be created to specification. For details, contact specialsales@abramsbooks.com or the address below.

ABRAMS The Art of Books
195 Broadway, New York, NY 10007
abramsbooks.com

THE CONCEPT

We, at Cereal, have traveled to cities around the world and sought out places we believe to be unique, interesting, and enjoyable. Our aim is to produce guides that would befit Cereal readers and modern travelers alike, recommending a tightly edited selection of experiences that combine quality with meticulous design. If the food is top-notch, so too is the space that accompanies it. You'll soon notice that our version of the perfect trip is woven in with an understated flair and a penchant for grand landscapes, both natural and constructed. Within these pages, you will find the practical advice you need on where to stay, where to eat, what to see, and where to shop.

THE GUIDE

This guide to Copenhagen features a considered selection of shops, hotels, restaurants, cafés, and points of interest. Not intending to be comprehensive, we present a discerning edit of our favorite places to visit in the city.

All photographs, copy, and illustrations are original and exclusive to Cereal.

While all information in this book was accurate at the time of printing, please call venues before visiting to confirm that nothing has changed.

CONTENTS

A City Guide by CEREAL

INTERVIEWS

ESSAYS

ADDITIONAL INFORMATION

COPENHAGEN

Perched on the eastern edge of Sjælland island and linked to Malmö in Sweden by the soaring Øresund Bridge, Copenhagen is the birthplace of New Nordic Cuisine and home to Hans Christian Anderson's legacy of fairytales. While other cities are embodied by towers, castles or palaces, the Danish capital sports a twentieth-century bronze statue of a mermaid, barely four feet high: understatement is the hallmark of this center of world class design. But if all the clean lines get to be too much, head for the whirling opulence of the Tivoli Gardens, or venture into nature. Copenhagen has perfected a lifestyle for every season.

COUNTRY	DENMARK
AIRPORT	CPH
LANGUAGE	DANISH
CURRENCY	DKK
DIALING CODE	+45

A PHOTO ESSAY

photos by ASH JAMES

NEIGHBORHOODS

MAP
of COPENHAGEN

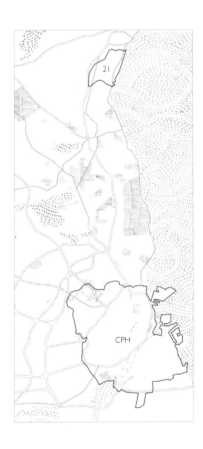

PLACES TO VISIT

HOTEL SANDERS

Set behind the Royal Danish Theater, Hotel Sanders—founded by former ballet dancer Alexander Kølpin—has a fitting air of theatricality. The in-house cocktail bar, TATA, is named for the red curtain used between performances at the nearby theater. Velvet curtains feature throughout the interiors, designed by Lind + Almond, which blend mid-century modern elements, rattan, and potted plants. With a lounge, courtyard, and roof terrace to relax in, Hotel Sanders has everything required for an intimate and memorable stay.

+45 46 40 00 40
hotelsanders.com

Tordenskjoldsgade 15
1055 Copenhagen

THE AUDO

HOTEL
in NORDHAVNEN

The Audo occupies the old merchant house of a shipping magnate, which Norm Architects have transformed into an immaculate ten-room boutique hotel, with a café, co-working space, and concept store. Furniture by Menu mixes with carefully curated vintage pieces, and commissions from artists such as Portland-based Benjamin Ewing. The Audo has a serene and welcoming atmosphere, which incites creative conversations and encounters.

+45 31 26 30 80
theaudo.com

Århusgade 130
2150 Copenhagen

HOTEL DANMARK

HOTEL
in CITY CENTER

Cozy and central, Hotel Danmark is no less sumptuous for the compact size of its rooms, which range from bunk rooms sleeping six to doubles with balconies. The hotel occupies an eighteenth-century building and its adjoining 1960s neighbor—distinctive at street level thanks to its glossy, green-tiled façade—with a courtyard garden and rooftop terrace squeezed in. The interiors are inspired by the rich color palette of the Thorvaldsens Museum, located just a short walk away, across the canal. Breakfast is organic, with *smørrebrød* for lunch.

+45 33 11 48 06
brochner-hotels.com/hotel-danmark

Vester Voldgade 89
1552 Copenhagen

NOBIS

The 1903 building that was once the Royal Danish Academy of Music has been home to Nobis Hotel since 2017. Spread over four floors, the hotel was designed by Wingårdh Architects, who have married its sweeping proportions with Scandinavian mid-century and contemporary furnishings—including ultra-comfortable DUX beds—all sandwiched between oak herringbone floors and elaborate stucco ceilings. The restaurant, Noi, led by Fredrik Sandberg, fuses Nordic ingredients with European influences, and offers everything from casual small plates to a full tasting menu.

+45 78 74 14 00
nobishotel.dk

Niels Brocks Gade 1
1574 Copenhagen

ALOUETTE

Alouette is not so much rooted in any one cuisine, but rather in the illustrious past of its head chef, Nick Curtin, who hails from gastronomic strongholds such as Almanak and Acme. The fixed, five-course menu changes constantly according to season, and there's no question that the restaurant warrants a trip to the Islands Brygge harborfront. Københavns Møbelsnedkeri oversaw the design of the converted pencil factory, from the volcanic stone floors to the custom wooden furniture and intensely red bathroom, which is evocative of Mark Frost and David Lynch's *Twin Peaks*.

+45 31 67 66 06
restaurant-alouette.dk

Sturlasgade 14P, 1
2300 Copenhagen

ALOUETTE RESTAURANT

ILUKA

RESTAURANT
in CITY CENTER

Visiting Iluka is the closest you can get to diving into the Baltic Sea without getting your clothes wet. Named after the Australian Aboriginal word *iluka*, which translates to "by the sea," Iluka's offering is exactly that: Its à la carte menu ranges from sea urchin sourced near the Faroe Islands and potted octopus, to the market fish of the day—all plated in an almost spartan fashion, with a subtle touch of Scandinavian refinement.

+45 30 30 95 89
restaurantiluka.dk

Peder Skrams Gade 15
1054 Copenhagen

YAFFA

This Israeli restaurant specializes in comfort food that's ideal for sharing around the table, with plenty of fresh herbs, hummus, eggplant caviar, falafel, and lamb. Warm and tactile, the space was designed by Copenhagen-based design studio Frama, with simple wooden chairs and benches, granite tabletops, and a curvy bar decked with abstract paintings in earthy tones. Yaffa's mix of bespoke Frama designs and Scandinavian classics, such as Alvar Aalto's 69 chair, gives the space a relaxed feel to match the menu.

+45 71 72 66 11
yaffa.dk

Gråbrødretorv 16 Kld
1154 Copenhagen

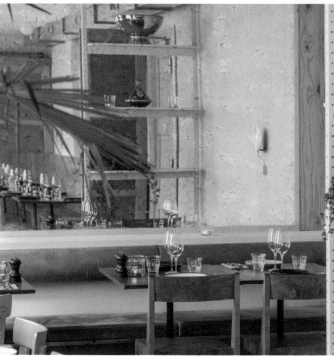

BÆST

Bæst's legendary pizzas, small courses, and à la carte dishes reflect the best daily produce from Christian F. Puglisi's Farm of Ideas, located just 30 miles away. This easy going restaurant sets the bar high: top class mozzarella made from organic milk, perfect pizza crusts made from local flour, and charcuterie from the finest Danish livestock; ingredients are certified 60–90% organic, and everything is prepared from scratch. While Bæst takes ample inspiration from Italy, it's pure Nørrebro at heart.

Read Christian F. Puglisi's essay on Copenhagen (see page 174)

+45 35 35 04 63
baest.dk

Guldbergsgade 29
2200 Copenhagen

AMASS

Pass canals, houseboats, and fields on your rented bike on a bright summer evening, and arrive at this muralled restaurant, domain of chef Matt Orlando. With a menu inspired by the vegetables, edible flowers, and herbs growing in the garden, combined with traditions such as fried chicken served alfresco on summer weekends, Orlando has created a unique offering within Copenhagen's dining landscape.

+45 43 58 43 30
amassrestaurant.com

Refshalevej 153
1432 Copenhagen

ADMIRALGADE 26

RESTAURANT
in CITY CENTER

The playfully erudite tone of Admiralgade 26's menu is a good indication of the experiences to follow: Dishes boast clean flavors, indulgent ingredients, and influences both Scandinavian and Asian, expertly balanced and prepared. The restaurant is by the same team behind Ved Stranden 10, and all wines on the discerning list can be served by the glass. In addition to the restaurant's impeccable and relaxed style of hospitality, the space is inhabited by the designs of Jean Prouvé, Alvar Aalto, and Michael Thonet and, naturally, is beloved by Copenhagen's creative set.

+45 33 33 79 73
admiralgade26.dk

Admiralgade 26
1066 Copenhagen

APOLLO BAR & KANTINE

Apollo Bar & Kantine is a relaxed and economical source of fresh food, led by renowned Copenhagen chef Frederik Bille Brahe, and a sociable place for evening drinks. Sheltered from the busier tourist tracts, the café shares the same ivy-strewn seventeenth-century building as the Kunsthal Charlottenborg—the contemporary exhibition space of the Royal Danish Academy of Fine Arts. In the summer, the outdoor tables at the edge of the courtyard will beckon, whether you're stopping by for an early coffee or at the start of a long, warm evening.

+45 60 53 44 14
apollobar.dk

Charlottenborg Palace, Nyhavn 2
1051 Copenhagen

VED STRANDEN 10

An enticing selection of natural wines, and a much sought after location by the canals of the city center, make Ved Stranden 10 one of the most popular wine bars in town. Wine connoisseurs and novices alike are welcomed in a warm and elegant setting, and concepts such as Monday Meals and Wednesday Tastings help to keep midweek evenings lively.

+45 35 42 40 40
vedstranden10.dk

Ved Stranden 10
1061 Copenhagen

SLURP

Founded by former Noma chef Philipp Inreiter, this small ramen joint can be found off a side street by the lakes that separate the city center from Nørrebro. Visit for some of the best ramen in town.

+45 53 70 80 83
slurpramen.dk

Nansensgade 90
1366 Copenhagen

EDAMAME & HORSERADISH 45
KIMCHI 45
KOREAN FRIED CHICKEN 80
SEE SPECIALS SELECTION

SHIO RAMEN 140
SHOYU RAMEN 140
VEGGIE RAMEN 135
MISO RAMEN 140

KAFETERIA

Kafeteria is the café at SMK, the country's largest art museum. The culinary focus is on local produce; breakfast is served with pastries en masse, and lunch with freshly baked bread and seasonal greens. Situated in the brightly lit portion of the museum built in the late nineteenth-century, Kafeteria was designed by Danish artist Danh Võ, with references to Scandinavian, Italian, and Japanese culture.

+45 60 52 46 96
kafeteriasmk.dk

SMK, Sølvgade 48–50
1307 Copenhagen

JUNO THE BAKERY

BAKERY
in ØSTERBRO

You can watch the pastries being made and emerging fresh from the oven in this tiny bakery. Don't be daunted by the inevitable queue: Short of securing one of its four seats, Juno's delectable pastries are best taken to go. Stock up on sticky cardamom buns, melt-in-the-mouth pistachio croissants, and, when in season, cream-filled semla. Not to be overshadowed by the array of more indulgent treats, the bread is equally worth trying. Walk across town to the harbor and enjoy your spoils by the water.

Århusgade 48
2100 Copenhagen

JUNO THE BAKERY BAKERY

LILLE BAKERY

CAFÉ & BAKERY
in REFSHALEØEN

The industrial structures on the island of Refshaleøen—a twenty-minute bike ride from the city center—formerly served as shipyard buildings. Now, they are home to a wealth of gastronomic destinations, one of them being Lille: An artisanal bakery inside an old, high-lofted brick building, serving breakfast and lunch, developed in close collaboration with local farmers. Delicacies on offer include custard-filled Berliners, sausage rolls, and homemade sourdough bread.

lillebakery.com

Refshalevej 213A
1432 Copenhagen

SESAME
SEED
12.-

COFFEE COLLECTIVE

CAFÉ
in NØRREBRO

The Coffee Collective has enjoyed both domestic and international success since launching their Direct Trade model, cutting out all intermediaries and dealing directly with coffee plant farmers. Their popular location on cobblestoned Jægersborggade in Nørrebro attracts a creative crowd, and conversations flow around the wooden tables. Swing by for an afternoon sweet treat—the cinnamon swirls from Meyers Bakery are a must-try.

+45 60 15 15 25
coffeecollective.dk

Jægersborggade 57
2200 Copenhagen

COFFEE COLLECTIVE CAFÉ

ØSTERBERG

Cathrine Østerberg has a combined love for ice cream and food science, and her frosty creations are homemade from start to finish. Inspired by her travels, the counter offers flavors such as jackfruit, tamarind, and durian, alongside more traditional options. There is also a second Østerberg location in Vesterbro.

Please note, Østerberg is only open during the summer months.

+45 61 42 32 89
osterberg-ice.dk

Rosenvængets Allé 7C
2100 Copenhagen

STUDIO OLIVER GUSTAV

INTERIORS SHOP
in ØSTERBRO

Creative consultant Oliver Gustav furnishes his monochrome boutique with eclectic pieces, in addition to his studio's own collections. Located in a former art museum on Kastelsvej, the space, atmospherically lit by the building's original skylights, is a beautiful environment that expresses Gustav's passion and aptitude for the fusion of art and design.

Cereal talks to Oliver Gustav (see page 152)

+45 27 37 46 30
studio.olivergustav.com

Kastelsvej 18
2100 Copenhagen

FRAMA

+45 31 40 60 30
framacph.com

Fredericiagade 57
1310 Copenhagen

In their interiors shop and design studio, Frama has preserved the original features of the building's former incarnation as a nineteenth-century pharmacy. Stripped back, raw textures and materials—marble, wood, plaster and rusted metal—are elevated by darker hues and moody, seclusive spaces. The furniture collection does not interrupt the sense of potential in the sparse decor, and homewares include a minimalist lighting collection and simple ceramics.

Read Niels Strøyer Christophersen's essay on Copenhagen (see page 168)

THE APARTMENT

Set in a beautifully restored eighteenth-century apartment overlooking the canals of Christianshavn, this combined showroom and shop is designed to feel like a Copenhagen home. Unique pieces from established and emerging designers are displayed alongside vintage items in the ground-floor space, creating a colorful and sophisticated composition. Above the store, on the fourth floor, The Apartment Residence is available for overnight stays. The space is designed by owner Tina Seidenfaden Busck, and includes hand-picked furniture from her private collection.

+45 31 62 04 02
theapartment.dk

Overgaden neden Vandet 33
1414 Copenhagen

YŌNOBI

A true ceramics aficionado, Nanna Egebjerg has traveled the world acquainting herself with local ceramicists and artists, collecting unique pieces from Los Angeles, Japan, southern France, and Denmark for her store in Copenhagen. Yōnobi—which translates as "beauty in practical objects" in Japanese—is an intimate space with serene concrete floors and steps, channeling a quiet mood. A three-minute cycle away is Yōnobi's ceramics studio, which holds daytime and evening classes in wheel-throwing, sculpture, and modeling for budding potters.

+45 71 99 41 90
itsyonobi.com

Løvstræde 1
1152 Copenhagen

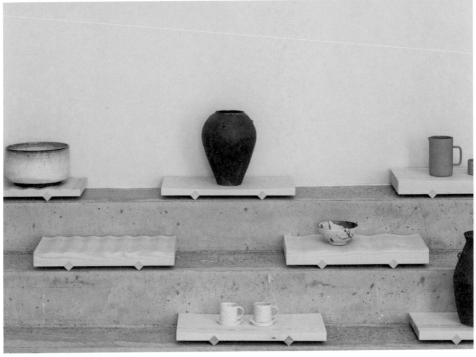

STUDIO X VIADUCT

Located close to the city's traditional gallery strip on Bredgade, this collaborative venture of Studio X director, Kirstine Meier Carlsen, and London-based showroom Viaduct, features examples of Danish and international furniture, objects, and lighting, in a space that's intended to feel comfortable and lived-in. The display is constantly evolving, with creators such as Alessi, e15, Flos, Valerie Objects, and Zanotta showcasing their designs here.

+45 31 51 62 72
studioxviaduct.com

Dronningens Tværgade 50
1302 Copenhagen

AIAYU

Aiayu (pronounced "ai-ya-yu") was one of the first sustainable design brands to be founded in Denmark. With an emphasis on knitwear and organic cotton, Aiayu's production supports growth and community development in Bolivia and India. The Copenhagen store, located just off the picturesque—albeit busy— streets of Nyhavn in the very heart of the city, affirms the brand's emphasis on quality, reflected in their clothing, cushions, throws, and ceramics, all made to last a lifetime.

+45 27 84 09 63
aiayu.com

Store Strandstræde 12A
1255 Copenhagen

AURE STUDIO

APPAREL & ACCESSORIES
in CITY CENTER

The result of four friends coming together from various crafts, Aure Studio is a multidisciplinary studio that transcends the spheres of design, fashion and art. Located only a stone's throw away from Copenhagen Botanical Garden, Aure Studio is open on Saturdays and select Sundays. The premises has an atmosphere of intimacy and a finely curated selection of clothing, apothecary, art and sculpture, placed thoughtfully throughout the space.

+45 27 12 01 23
aurestudio.com

Linnésgade 27
1361 Copenhagen

Aure—

objects, garments, visuals

NY CARLSBERG GLYPTOTEK

The Glyptotek was opened to the public in 1897 by one of Denmark's greatest art patrons Carl Jacobsen, of the family behind Carlsberg. Funded by his profits from beer-brewing, the Glyptotek holds an impressive collection of marble masterpieces, art, and antiquities, spanning six thousand years of art history. Enter through the Winter Garden—where fountains, palm trees, and the museum eatery, Picnic, reside below a glass dome ceiling—and continue through the magnificent rooms painted in warm reds, yellows, and blues.

+45 33 41 81 41
glyptoteket.dk

Dantes Plads 7
1556 Copenhagen

NY CARLSBERG GLYPTOTEK MUSEUM

129

LOUISIANA MUSEUM

MUSEUM
in HUMLEBÆK

To the north of Copenhagen, overlooking the Øresund Sound, is the striking Louisiana Museum of Modern Art. Opened in 1958, the clean horizontal lines and wide glazing of the mid-century extension connect the building to the surrounding gardens and coastline. The museum derives its name from the first owner of the property, whose three wives were all named Louise. It is among the most visited art museums in Denmark, and remains one of the world's most respected exhibition venues.

+45 49 19 07 19
louisiana.dk

Gammel Strandvej 13
3050 Humlebæk

ASSISTENS CEMETERY

POINT OF INTEREST
in NØRREBRO

Certain pastimes that may seem odd to out-of-towners can be a given to Copenhageners, such as taking a break from the bustling center in one of the city's largest cemeteries, bringing lunch or wine, soaking up the sun, and taking a nap in the grass. In the heart of Nørrebro is the Assistens Cemetery, serving as the final resting place for icons such as author Hans Christian Andersen, philosopher Søren Kierkegaard, and jazz musician Ben Webster. Go for a walk down its tree-lined avenue or find a spot in the shade to rest and unwind before venturing out into the city once more.

+45 35 37 19 17
assistens.dk

Kapelvej 4
2200 Copenhagen

RUNDETAARN

Providing very splendid views over the city, Rundetaarn—Round Tower—was originally built as an observatory in the seventeenth century. Its spiralling brick corridors were used to transport heavy equipment with horse-drawn wagons. Today, the tower stands as the oldest functioning observatory in Europe, and is attached to the University of Copenhagen Library and Trinitatis Church.

+45 33 73 03 73
rundetaarn.dk

Københavnergade 52A
1150 Copenhagen

RUNDETAARN POINT OF INTEREST

GRUNDTVIG'S CHURCH

POINT OF INTEREST
in NORDVEST

Grundtvig's Church sits on top of a small hill. The name of the church's location—På Bjerget—means "on the mountain." Built between 1921 and 1940, this architectural gem commemorates Evangelical Lutheran preacher N.F.S. Grundtvig, who presented his church with a new perspective: human first, Christian second.

+45 35 81 54 42
grundtvigskirke.dk

På Bjerget 14B
2400 Copenhagen

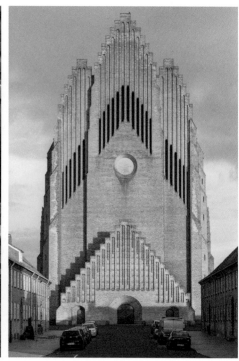

ANDERSEN & MAILLARD

ADDITIONAL RECOMMENDATIONS

RADISSON COLLECTION ROYAL HOTEL *Hotel | radissonhotels.com*

HOTEL OTTILIA *Hotel | brochner-hotels.com/hotel-ottilia*

NOMA *Restaurant | noma.dk*

MANGIA *Restaurant | mangia.dk*

LA BANCHINA *Restaurant | labanchina.dk*

ANDERSEN & MAILLARD *Bakery | andersenmaillard.dk*

CAFÉ ATELIER SEPTEMBER *Café | cafeatelierseptember.com*

BRUS *Brewery & Bakery | tapperietbrus.dk*

DEN VANDRETTE *Wine Bar | denvandrette.dk*

NEW WORKS STUDIO *Showroom | newworks.dk*

DANSK MADE FOR ROOMS *Homewares Shop | danskshop.com*

STILLEBEN *Homewares Shop | stilleben.dk*

DANSK MADE FOR ROOMS

BÆST

STILLEBEN

INTERVIEWS

THE CASE FOR GRAY:
AN INTERVIEW WITH OLIVER GUSTAV

words by OLLIE HORNE

photos by ASH JAMES

"I am very fond of the special Nordic light we have up here," says Oliver Gustav. In his Østerbro showroom and studio, it floods in through the skylights, cold and soft, illuminating the gray walls, cornices, and doorways in a manner not dissimilar to the subdued interiors of Danish painter Vilhelm Hammershøi (1864–1916). "I often refer to his paintings," says Gustav. "He was also drawn to the quality of the light here. My interiors are always monochrome, but by playing with the shadows and the light, I give them a kind of chromatism."

Although the designer and creative consultant's muted palette and reverence for light are indeed reminiscent of Hammershøi, Gustav's spaces differ in that they are filled with objects. His Copenhagen showroom—a 1920s former art museum on Kastelsvej—houses an eclectic array of sculptural metal chairs, sofas upholstered in thick white linen, ancient stoneware, and found fragments of metal and wood that, in this context, acquire the presence of rarefied art objects.

Studio Oliver Gustav held a show of Hammershøi's work in September 2019, presenting three of his paintings alongside their carefully arranged displays. The event ran for four days and each night, the paintings—dating from the year 1900—had to be taken down and stored in a safety box for their protection. Gustav's fondness for Hammershøi began ten years earlier, when he was renovating an eighteeth-century palazzo in Frederiksstaden, central Copenhagen, which would become his apartment and studio. The building's listed status meant little could be done to the interiors, to the extent that the local government had prescribed

See page 98 for information on Studio Oliver Gustav

an official color scheme for the property: "I was allowed to use a very bright blue, and a strong red," he laughs. Given that Gustav's interiors rarely deviate from his strict gray palette ("the shades are constantly changing, just not the colors," he tells me), this condition was, understandably, not to his liking. "I took a chance: I made a few tests in grayish tones on the walls, and created a little presentation about Hammershøi and his interiors. In the end, they allowed me to go ahead with my color scheme, inspired by his work. I think, from that point on, I have been very much in love with his paintings."

Like the painter, Gustav was born in Copenhagen, and has lived his whole adult life in the city, founding his studio here in 2009. He describes himself as a creative consultant in aesthetics, art, and interior design, and is known for pairing the work of contemporary designers, such as Faye Toogood, Rick Owens, and Vincenzo De Cotiis, with pieces from his own collection, as well as antiquities and other artworks. His job regularly takes him overseas—at the time of writing, he is working on a home in St. Barts—but he enjoys his quiet, peaceful life at home in Copenhagen. He lives five minutes away from the studio and showroom in Østerbro, which he walks to every day with his dog, a shaggy, gray poodle named Emma. "I am a very private person, and need time to reload," he says. "We do not work on more than two or three projects a year, because I don't want to. My work is a love story: I love doing these projects, and I devote all my energy to them."

Another important love story for Gustav is the city itself. "Copenhagen is such a beautiful little town," he says. "I enjoy knowing every corner of it. And so much is happening here these days in terms of culture and food." But crucially, it is Copenhagen's historic architecture that has the greatest hold on him: "I have always been drawn to old Danish architecture," he says. "There are so many details in these buildings: the doorways, the frames, the cornicing. That's why I always paint in monochrome. I don't want any one part to stand out too much. If everything is one color the details blur in a beautiful way, creating a silent, peaceful environment."

The case in point is his showroom, where each of the ten rooms is painted a different tranquil, earthy shade. Gustav bought the space in 2016, and was ready to open one month later. "I really like doing things myself, so my team and I worked on it together—and we are very effective," he laughs. "I like to be hands on. I am always painting or getting involved in metalwork." His partner joined the team of eight as CEO in 2018, cementing what feels to Gustav like a little family. "It is very cozy," he says. "We are preparing for Christmas right now, so my team is using free half-hours here and there to make decorations at their desks."

The final piece of the puzzle, his love of objects, comes from rather further afield than Copenhagen. His great-grandfather, who spent more than twenty years living in Vietnam, was a voracious collector of ancient objects and sculptures. Gustav never got to meet him, but his grandfather, as the only child, inherited the collection. "My grandfather always had a curious eye," Gustav says. "I remember him showing me these dense photo albums of my great-grandfather in Vietnam, posing with crocodiles and things. I loved the storytelling about this other era, and was intrigued by everything he kept on display. My grandfather opened my eyes to beautiful things."

"I want to find beauty in simple, basic forms," he says. "For instance, I recently found the fragment of a door from an old liquor store in Texas, with a peephole in it. For me, it became this wonderful art object, so I hung it on the wall. I love collecting found objects like this. It is almost a religion for me—to live a beautiful life, as simply as possible."

STUDIO.OLIVERGUSTAV.COM

EASE & HERITAGE:
AN INTERVIEW WITH CECILIE BAHNSEN

words by NIKOLAJ HANSSON
photos by IRINA BOERSMA
styling by PERNILLE VEST

Conjuring the elegant femininity of Paris, the raw intensity of London and the democratic refinement of Copenhagen, Cecilie Bahnsen has shaped a new paradigm in the Scandinavian and global fashion spheres with her eponymous label. Having relocated back to her native Copenhagen after stints in Paris and London, Bahnsen shares her thoughts on the city she calls home, and its influence on her work.

CEREAL: You studied abroad in London and worked for some time in Paris, before moving back to Copenhagen to set up your brand. What prompted you to return?

CECILIE BAHNSEN: I moved back to Copenhagen because I needed a change of pace; time to adjust my focus and develop my own style, without being influenced by the hectic tempo and high expectations of the world's fashion capitals. I had an idea for a high-end fashion brand that expanded on Denmark's architectural and design heritage, and I wanted to explore whether this was really possible.

CEREAL: How does the character of the city inform your work?

CB: I want my universe to be feminine and modern, mixing emotions and inherent beauty with the openness, simplicity, and pragmatism that come from my Danish background. I look to the intricacy and romance of London and Paris for inspiration, juxtaposing these elements with the Scandinavian minimalism and ease that are more in line with my personal sentiments. Design needs to feel effortless to me, and Copenhagen has a very relaxed quality, which is reflected in its approach to fashion.

I am drawn to the freshness and purity of the different styles and flourishes of color that you see on the streets here. Something that is important for me to share with the Copenhagen girls who wear Cecilie Bahnsen is the need to feel comfortable. Some of our dresses can be worn to a party on the weekend and thrown back on when Monday comes round, simply because that's what you want to wear—nothing needs to be saved only for special occasions.

CEREAL: Do you have any particular rituals tied to the city when starting work on a new collection?

CB: During summertime, I go swimming in the sea before work. It really clears my head and gives me energy for the day ahead. I also love to begin my research and sketching at the Design Museum Danmark, with its extensive library and design archive.

CEREAL: When does Copenhagen feel most like home to you?

CB: To me, Copenhagen really comes alive in the summer. Everyone is outside, enjoying the sun and the nature around them. You bump into friends and family throughout the city and make the most of the long, bright days together. But there is also the feeling of home in fresh air, windy bike rides, and drinking coffee with friends outside, even when it is too cold to do so.

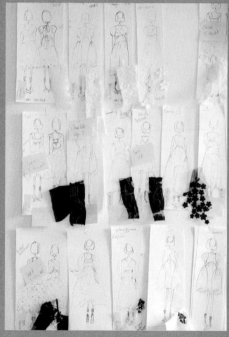

CEREAL: Which places would you say one has to visit when in Copenhagen?

CB: I recommend visiting the Louisiana Museum of Modern Art north of the city for its art, architecture, and scenic views, and Galleri Nicolai Wallner for a well-curated selection of contemporary art. Café Atelier September is a lovely place for breakfast, as is Admiralgade 26 for lunch, and the Pescetarian for dinner. Studio X Viaduct and Hay House are my choices for interior shopping, and Holly Golightly for fashion.

CEREAL: What do you think makes Copenhagen stand out among other European capitals?

CB: Its panoramic views and the openness of the city; you're always close to the sea and none of the houses are built very high, so you always feel a freshness and lightness in the air when exploring Copenhagen.

———

CECILIEBAHNSEN.COM

ESSAYS

MY COPENHAGEN

by NIELS STRØYER CHRISTOPHERSEN

photos by IRINA BOERSMA

Niels Strøyer Christophersen is the founder of Frama, a Copenhagen design studio that creates honest furniture, homewares, and interiors with an emphasis on simple forms and raw materiality. He moved to Copenhagen after graduating from high school, and has lived and worked in the city ever since. His home is in an old watchmaker's shop, which he has gradually restored.

Copenhagen has changed dramatically since I arrived here in 2003, but at the same time, I feel the city is very much the same; it still has a small village feel about it. It is like Brooklyn, or East London: There are parts that are busier or quieter than others, but it is essentially one big neighborhood. It makes you feel at home. You are not one in ten million here.

I live in Østerbro, which is a very green area. I have a beautiful bike ride to work every day to the Frama space in Nyboder. If Copenhagen is a small village, then Nyboder is the village inside the village. People tend to overlook the area; there's not really a reason to go there except perhaps for a stroll, even though it is so central in Copenhagen K. I cycle through Kastellet, the star-shaped fort, which is a very peaceful place; the English Church is near there, a beautifully located and decorated monument, and the Little Mermaid sculpture is nearby at the water's edge.

I grew up about an hour's drive away, in Næstved. Denmark is small, so even a short distance can feel like a different world. I moved to Copenhagen just after graduating from high school. It wasn't really a question—the place was full of possibility and opportunity. In a way, it felt bigger then, as so much of it was still unknown to me. I moved in with my aunt, who was living about a fifteen-minute cycle from the center, in Utterslev. The house was

See page 102 for information on Frama

in a quiet neighborhood not far from Grundtvig's Church, which is an amazing building, designed by Peder Vilhelm Jense-Klint, and finished by his son Kaare Klint, who is often referred to as the father of Danish design. It is constructed in beautiful yellow bricks, and all the residential buildings around it were built at the same time in the same brick.

During this time, I started working for a small construction company, which is how I first became familiar with Copenhagen: navigating its various districts, picking up building materials, and delivering them to different projects around the city. I also learned to understand the skeleton of a building, to see its spaces without interiors or decoration—to appreciate its raw beauty. This has become a major theme in Frama: appreciating the nature of the materials we work with. I think for all of us, these different periods of our life, whatever they may be and however brief they are, end up affecting us somehow.

I went through a process of moving a handful of times, until 2011, when I found the apartment in Østerbro—in an old watchmaker's shop—that I live in to this day. It offered me the quietude I was looking for. Østerbro is filled with large residential buildings from the late-nineteenth and early-twentieth centuries; they're not built so on top of one another, so the neighborhood feels spacious. When I found my home, it had been empty for two years or more, and hadn't been modernized for at least fifty. It met all of my criteria: It was at street level, with high ceilings, in an alternative, unconventional space. I bought it and began renovating.

It was an emotional time for me—I had just started Frama and was going through changes in my personal life. I invested a lot of energy in the apartment. I had no plan, I just went with solutions that felt natural, intuitive, and simple. For example, I removed a door that was joining the sitting room and bedroom, and instead of replacing it with a plaster wall, I fitted two glass panes over the gap. It allows light to pass through the space, and reveals the inner wall and the wooden frame of the doorway. You can see the construction of the

building. I really like this about the apartment, and it is a quality shared by Frama as well: You can understand what is going on with the design just by looking.

The Frama space has moved about the city, too. I started in Hellerup before moving to Nordhavnen—an industrial area that is undergoing a huge development. We were there for some years. It suited us, but the space began to define us too narrowly as an industrial brand—we are more than that, we are refined and elegant as well. We decided to move out when the development started, and after a brief period being based out of my apartment, I came across the old pharmacy in Nyboder. It avoided any easy definition: It was ornamental and sophisticated; it had a sense of heritage, with the original wood shelving still in place, but it also had some backrooms that felt fresh and modern. It meant we could present the juxtapositions inherent in our brand: hard and soft, masculine and feminine, clean and tactile. We are not inventing anything new at Frama; we are interested in essential forms, some of which have existed since ancient Egyptian times. Our offering is the thought surrounding the object. The philosophy, the ethos—that is our design.

There is probably a strong subconscious connection between living in Copenhagen and what Frama aims to express. We work with an appreciation for a global market and the different cultures and people of the world, yet our core way of thinking is very Danish. As a company, we are open-minded, international, and welcoming. These values go hand in hand with the city of Copenhagen.

———
FRAMACPH.COM

MY COPENHAGEN

by CHRISTIAN F. PUGLISI

photo by CHRIS TONNESEN

Chef Christian F. Puglisi is an unstoppable force, and has revolutionized the gastronomy scene in Copenhagen through his diverse, organic eateries and 48-hectare (120 acre) organic farm. His restaurants include Mirabelle and Bæst, along with wine supplier Vinikultur, and vermouth bar Rudo.

I was born in Sicily but came to Denmark with my parents when I was eight years old. I've since traveled, working in Spain and France, but returned to Copenhagen in 2007. It feels like home— it's been my home since 1990, when we first moved here.

When I started out as a chef apprentice, Copenhagen wasn't the city to stay in. Everyone ambitious in those years was taking off, going to new places to learn. It never felt like you could reach the same world-class level if you stayed in Denmark—it was much too provincial. Today, it's become almost the opposite. A lot of people travel to Copenhagen for work, and it's a real center for gastronomy.

The New Nordic food movement, started by Noma, has had its moment—not in a negative way, it's just how things go. It was a very important part of helping people to understand and appreciate that eating local is also possible in this part of the world. The next step is to focus on the sustainability of local foods. To me, "local" is not a question of geography, but one of values. My passion for organic produce was ignited when I became a father in 2011. Until then, the concept of quality had been about aesthetics and taste— the radishes being very small and attractive, or the flesh of the fish being plump. But I started thinking of food as nourishment, and became more aware of a holistic approach to eating and connecting pleasure not only with nourishment, but with the ecosystem from which food is sourced.

See page 54 for information on Puglisi's restaurant, Bæst

We established a farm about forty-five minutes outside Copenhagen in 2016. The idea was to take greater steps towards understanding the produce we were using. Now, the produce takes first priority—it decides what you end up cooking. On a creative level, it's an interesting challenge. We started out just wanting to grow some vegetables, but we've added cows, and we've had pigs, chickens, rabbits, ducks, and laying hens. I know for a fact that farming isn't easy. I don't think we, as chefs, can possibly be better at growing a carrot than someone who has grown carrots their entire life, but I think the contribution we can make to agriculture as gastronomists is very relevant.

Copenhagen has a lightness that other cities don't have. I live in Nørrebro—five hundred yards from Bæst—and it feels like a village. It's the perfect combination of being close to the action but not being overwhelmed. You don't get the same feeling you do in London or New York—both cities I adore—which feel suffocating after a couple of days, as though they take something away from you. Here, you are close to the water, within twenty minutes you can see a forest and be in nature, and wherever you are in the city, it's so easy to move around. Bike lanes are well organized, pedestrian traffic makes sense, and cars aren't what they are in other big cities.

I believe to feel inspired is to be in a good place, surrounded by positivity and people who enjoy themselves. This city has a lot to give and is generous in many ways, even though it's in Scandinavia and in the fall and winter everything is a bit rainy and dark. But these times also offer something: coziness. When there's not much light, you need to lighten up your day with other things. Copenhageners are quite good at doing that.

When visiting Copenhagen, one should give oneself time to escape the city. It's so seamless here. You can go to the coast or the countryside without any hassle. In the last couple of years, water has become more central to Copenhagen. The harbors have been cleaned up and there's a real culture around the water that I don't recall from even five years ago. People jump in the harbor and do all sorts of water sports around the city, and I think that's really special. It's not Barcelona—it will never be as hot—but somehow it doesn't really matter if you have the right spirit.

PUGLISI.DK

JOY IN DESIGN:
FINN JUHL'S HOUSE

words by RUTH AINSWORTH
photos by ALICE GAO

Finn Juhl's house, which the designer and architect built for himself and his first wife, speaks eloquently of the coherence and confidence of its creator's vision. Most significantly known for his progressive furniture design, in which he was famously self-taught, Finn Juhl is among the most celebrated of mid-century Danish designers; the restrained, supple forms of his pieces now a requisite in the modern vocabulary of interior design.

The house's character is one of satisfactory repose, each object resting comfortably in its place. Perhaps this is because, conceptually, the rooms were built around these items, and the building, in its turn, around the rooms. Sculptures, paintings, chairs, and tables, like the one-story house itself, form one low, undulating level, spreading a quality of even calm from one area of the house to the next. Light is warming or cooling at Juhl's command: diffused by sheer white curtains or a milky glass lampshade, reflected from white walls, or absorbed by a cream ceiling or dark wooden table.

The paintings, characterized by expressive rhythm and restricted, complementary palettes, describe art's influence for Juhl on this most personal of projects. Colors and forms bounce in musical reference to one another and coexist within a flowing composition where division is absent and color flourishes, shifting to articulate transitions and modulate spaces. Even a vivid jade chair or a hot pink rug declines to shout above the neutral white and wooden bones of the interior; rather, every element of the house engages in quiet, intelligent conversation with the others, never interrupting or disrupting, yet always holding its own. Juhl's hedonistic brand

of utilitarianism finds joy in every object, whether functional or decorative, from a simple soup bowl to a curving white chimney breast, from a contoured elbow rest to a polished wooden sculpture, establishing a democracy of objects built on a deep passion for form and design.

———

ORDRUPGAARD.DK/FINN-JUHLS-HUS

A LIVING EXAMPLE:
VIPP CHIMNEY HOUSE

words by NANA HAGEL
photos by ASH JAMES

Danish design company Vipp—best known for their steel pedal bin, first created in 1939—has, in recent years, set up the Vipp Hotel. In their playful interpretation, the hotel's "rooms" are entire properties, scattered across three locations in Sweden and Denmark. Following the Vipp Shelter in Lake Immeln, Sweden, and the Vipp Loft in Copenhagen, the third room is located in the Tuborg Harbor district just north of the city. Here, Danish architects Studio David Thulstrup have designed a contemporary home inside the shell of a 1902 water pumping station, altering everything but the striking red brick exterior and its original chimney of 115 feet. With the addition of a black-steel top floor, the rebuild has transformed the space into a two thousand-square-foot, two-level residence.

The ground floor includes industrial design pieces and materials such as concrete, steel, and stone, softened by terrazzo flooring and hues of orange, terra-cotta, and subdued pink. The Chimney Sofa, in burnt orange, looks out to the garden through arched windows. Intersecting the entire house is a dramatic steel staircase, clad in extruded aluminum paneling. The upstairs living area consists of two bedrooms, one with a walk-in closet and balcony, and a large bathroom. The rooms overlook the atrium, with a skylight view of the old chimney.

Studio David Thulstrup has brought new life to this heritage building. Chimney House is an extension of Vipp's existing universe; a modern home filled with living examples of its legacy.

———

VIPP.COM/HOTEL/VIPP-CHIMNEY-HOUSE

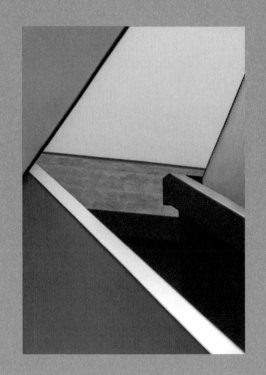

ADDITIONAL INFORMATION

ARCHITECTURE

POINTS OF INTEREST

1   GRUNDTVIG'S CHURCH

Peder Vilhelm Jensen-Klint and Kaare Klint, *1940*. På Bjerget 14B, 2400 Copenhagen.

2   RUNDETAARN

Hans van Steenwinckel the Younger, *1642*. Købmagergade 52A, 1150 Copenhagen.

3   SUPERKILEN PARK

Superflex, Bjarke Ingels Group & Topotek 1, *2012*. Nørrebrogade 210, 2200 Copenhagen.

4   THE ROYAL LIBRARY

Schmidt Hammer Lassen Architects, *1999*. Black Diamond, Søren Kierkegaards Plads 1, 1221, Copenhagen.

5   ORDRUPGAARD

Zaha Hadid, *2005*. Vilvordevej 110, 2920 Charlottenlund.

6   M/S MARITIME MUSEUM OF DENMARK

Bjarke Ingels Group, *2013*. Ny Kronborgvej 1, 3000 Helsingør.

7   COPENHAGEN OPERA HOUSE

Henning Larsen, *2004*. Ekvipagemestervej 10, 1438 Copenhagen K.

8   THE RADISSON COLLECTION ROYAL HOTEL

Arne Jacobsen, *1960*. Hammerichsgade 1, 1611 Copenhagen.

9   FREDERIK'S CHURCH

Nicolai Eigtved, Nicolas-Henri Jardin & Ferdinand Meldahl, *1894*. Frederiksgade 4, 1265 Copenhagen.

10   ROSENBORG CASTLE

Hans van Steenwinckel the Younger and Bertel Lange, *1624*. Øster Voldgade 4A, 1350 Copenhagen.

ART

POINTS OF INTEREST

1   NY CARLSBERG GLYPTOTEK

Art Museum, Dantes Plads 7, 1556 Copenhagen.

2   FINN JUHL'S HOUSE

Museum, Kratvænget 15, 2920 Charlottenlund.

3   LOUISIANA MUSEUM

Art Museum, Gl Strandvej 13, 3050 Humlebæk.

4   THORVALDSENS MUSEUM

Museum, Bertel Thorvaldsens Plads 2, 1213 Copenhagen K.

5   THE DAVID COLLECTION

Museum, Kronprinsessegade 30-32, 1306 Copenhagen.

6   SMK—THE NATIONAL GALLERY OF DENMARK

Gallery, Sølvgade 48-50, 1307 Copenhagen K.

7   HIRSCHSPRUNG COLLECTION

Museum, Stockholmsgade 20, 2100 Copenhagen.

8   COPENHAGEN CONTEMPORARY

Art Center, Refshalevej 173A, 1432 Copenhagen K.

9   GALLERY DANISH FURNITURE

Gallery, Bredgade 5, 1260 Copenhagen K.

10   KUNSTHAL CHARLOTTENBORG

Gallery, Kongens Nytorv 1, 1050 Copenhagen K.

SVINKLØV
BEACH HOTEL

RUDOLPH TEGNER
MUSEUM & STATUE PARK

COPENHAGEN

BORNHO

MØNS KLINT

ÆRØ ISLAND

N

WEEKEND TRIPS

33.5 miles (54 km)

RUDOLPH TEGNER MUSEUM & STATUE PARK
50 minutes by car, or 2 hours by train and bus.

For a cubic, concrete building with a surrounding sculpture park, built in 1937 by Danish symbolist sculptor Rudolph Tegner, in the midst of north Sjælland hills.

86 miles (139 km)

MØNS KLINT
2 hours by car.

For a four-mile stretch of white chalk cliffs on the eastern coast of Møn Island in the Baltic Sea, covered in woodlands, and designated a UNESCO biosphere.

114 miles (183 km)

BORNHOLM
4 hours and 20 minutes by car, 3 hours by bus, or 40 minutes by plane.

For gentle weather and rough geology, and visiting the medieval ruins of Hammershus, on an island in the Baltic Sea. Stay at Hotel Nordlandet and dine at Michelin-starred restaurant Kadeau, as well as the many smokehouses around the island.

120 miles (193 km)

THE MONICA, ÆRØ ISLAND
3 hours and 40 minutes by train and ferry, or 4 hours by car and ferry.

For a first-class experience of Danish island life at two-room boutique hotel the Monica, on the picturesque Ærø Island, in the South Funen Archipelago.

202.5 miles (326 km)

SVINKLØV BEACH HOTEL
4 hours and 50 minutes by car.

For a taste of simple Danish hospitality in a North Sea beach hotel, surrounded by rugged, unspoilt coastline, dunes, and forest.

THE CEREAL EDIT

1   HAND WASH & HAND LOTION
FROM FRAMA

The St. Pauls Apothecary Collection, named for the pharmacists who once occupied Frama's Nyboder store, is made in Copenhagen with natural, handpicked ingredients, including ylang-ylang, cedar, and sandalwood. The collection of soaps, lotions, conditioners, and perfumes all possess Frama's unique aroma, and are blended with essential oils. The collection is bottled in Italian colored glass, and is fittingly on display along the pharmacy's original shelving.

2   LINENS
FROM AIAYU

Sustainable-design brand Aiayu has a zero-waste program in place for all their cotton products sourced from India, including their collection of organic bed linen. Made from cotton poplin, the bed sheets, duvet covers, and pillowcases come in a range of neutral tones. Perusing the collection in its mineral gray store in Copenhagen K is sure to stir a longing for your bed at home, so pick a set to take back with you and make your awaited reunion all the sweeter.

3 PAINTER'S JACKET FROM AURE STUDIO

Aure is a multidisciplinary studio that creates garments, artworks, and interior design from their shop and studio in Copenhagen K. Their lightweight, cotton canvas jacket in cream or black, inspired by practical workwear, is an ideal layer for the changeable, in-between weather of Northern Europe, and as it's cut in a loose fit, it can suit all genders and body shapes.

4 LICORICE FROM LAKRIDS BY BÜLOW

Licorice, particularly the salty-sweet kind, is a favorite among Danes. Lakrids by Bülow, founded by Johan Bülow on his native island of Bornholm in 2007 (*lakrids* is the Danish word for "licorice"), sources the finest licorice root to make their treats, which come in sweet, salty, red, and habanero varieties, although the coated range is where the real excitement lies. Visit one of two central Copenhagen stores to try Bülow's signature: spheres of sweet licorice, coated in milk chocolate, with a dusting of licorice powder on the outside.

5 HK PITCHER FROM GEORG JENSEN

Georg Jensen began in 1904 as a small silversmithy at 36 Bredgade, Copenhagen. Now with locations in Frederiksberg and on the pedestrianized Strøget, Georg Jensen remains renowned for its silverware, jewelry, watches and homewares. The sleek, curving HK Pitcher in polished stainless steel was originally designed by Henning Koppel, and endures as a landmark of mid-century Danish design.

A DAY IN COPENHAGEN

AN ITINERARY

10 A.M. KAFETERIA

Start the day at Kafeteria, found inside SMK, the National Gallery of Denmark, for a coffee and a *morgenkomplet*—a breakfast plate of eggs, sourdough, and Havgus cheese. Before you leave, look around SMK and its collection of European art. *See page 78*

11 A.M. FRAMA

Visit the Frama studio a short walk away in the peaceful Nyboder neighborhood. Its St. Pauls Apothecary collection of soaps and lotions, as well as pieces from its furniture and homeware range, is presented within the store's layered, textural interior. *See page 102*

NOON STUDIO X VIADUCT

Walk five minutes down Adelgade to Studio X Viaduct and browse the selection of furniture, lighting, and homewares in an unfussy but nonetheless alluring and inspiring space. *See page 114*

1 P.M. RUNDETAARN

Take a stroll through verdant Kongens Have towards Rundetaarn—the Round Tower—built by Christian IV of Denmark in the seventeenth century as a royal observatory. Climb the spiraling ramp for views over the city. *See page 138*

2 P.M.   APOLLO BAR AND KANTINE

Head to Apollo Bar and Kantine for a light and simple lunch, and enjoy the Kunsthal Charlottenborg's beautiful courtyard. Mondays through Fridays, expect to be joined by students from the Academy of Fine Arts. *See page 66*

3 P.M.   YŌNOBI

After lunch, visit Yōnobi ceramics shop to browse handmade pieces selected from makers across the globe, including unique stoneware teapots, vases, and bowls, presented in calming and serene surroundings. *See page 110*

4 P.M.   NY CARLSBERG GLYPTOTEK

Spend the rest of the afternoon exploring nineteenth-century Danish and French paintings and marble sculptures from Ancient Egypt, Greece, and Italy in Ny Carlsberg Glyptotek, the independent art museum founded by Carl Jacobsen. The leafy Winter Garden is also a highlight. *See page 126*

7 P.M.   VED STRANDEN 10

Walk along the canal for a pre-dinner drink at Ved Stranden 10 wine bar, serving some of Copenhagen's finest natural wines in a cozy, living room atmosphere. *See page 70*

8 P.M.   ADMIRALGADE 26

Once your appetite has grown, head around the corner to Admiralgade 26 for dinner, run by the same team as Ved Stranden 10. Choose from either the à la carte menu, a selection of small plates, or a full-on tasting menu. *See page 62*

CEREAL PACKING TIPS

OUR SIX ESSENTIALS

TOTE BAG

A lightweight, foldable tote bag is handy when you buy one too many souvenirs and can't fit them all in your suitcase. It's also a great option for carrying your daily essentials as you explore the city.

SUPPLEMENTS

A small pillbox of supplements such as echinacea, vitamins, and Korean ginseng can prove useful when on the road. Jet lag and changes in temperature and environment can make you feel run-down. It's a good idea to give your immune system a boost!

SCARF

A large scarf will not only keep you warm when it's cold and protect you from the sun when it's hot; it will also double as a much-needed blanket on flights and train journeys. Choose the material of your scarf according to the time of year: linen for warmer months, and wool or cashmere for chillier weather.

SNEAKERS

A pair of good-looking sneakers that can be paired with any outfit, from morning to evening, is the uniform of many Copenhageners. The city is ideal for exploring on foot and by bike, so a comfortable pair of shoes is essential.

MUSIC

Download the Cereal Spotify playlist before you leave! It's the perfect companion for those long-haul flights, train rides, and road trips.

readcereal.com/playlist

ESSENTIAL OIL

An essential oil in your scent of choice is a must. Depending on the oil, it can be used as a moisturizer, facial cleanser, makeup remover, beard oil, bug repellent, and calming meditative ointment.

Rosa Park is cofounder and editor in chief of Cereal. She travels extensively for the magazine and was inspired to create a series of city guides that highlighted her favorite places to visit. Cereal is a biannual magazine known for its original take on design, style, and travel.